101
London
Travel
Tips

101 London Travel Tips

By
Anglotopia

Table of Contents

Introduction to the 2nd Edition

When we wrote the first edition of 101 London Travel Tips circa 2010, things were much different for London and for us. We were starting out as a business and London hadn't yet hosted the 2012 Olympics. A few months ago I was reading through the old book and realized that it was woefully out of date and needed an update.

We think of London as our second home. The idea of the original book came from various mishaps on the travels that we had while exploring this great city. We've traveled to London 20 times now, and we've learned something new on every trip.

This book will help you easily navigate through London's quirks. Keep in mind that as you travel you are, in fact, traveling. You have chosen a vacation to immerse yourself in a new culture. If you're open-minded and relaxed, you will have a wonderful time.

Tourists travel from around the globe to see the treasures that London holds. Make sure to get out and see the city. Take full advantage of all of the free attractions and fantastic parks. Take in a nice cup of tea at teatime or have a pint in a pub. Fully immerse yourself in the culture and you will have a fabulous time. We promise.

London is a unique melting pot of cultures and people. You will encounter people from across the globe in London. Some are the nicest people on Earth, and others leave something to be desired. Just be polite, and remember a smile goes a long way.

I'm writing this in the midst of the global Covid-19 pandemic, and many of us are missing London dearly. We don't know when we'll be going back but we know that, with this guidebook in hand, you will be London ready when you can!

Bon Voyage!

Jonathan and Jackie Thomas
Publishers
Anglotopia

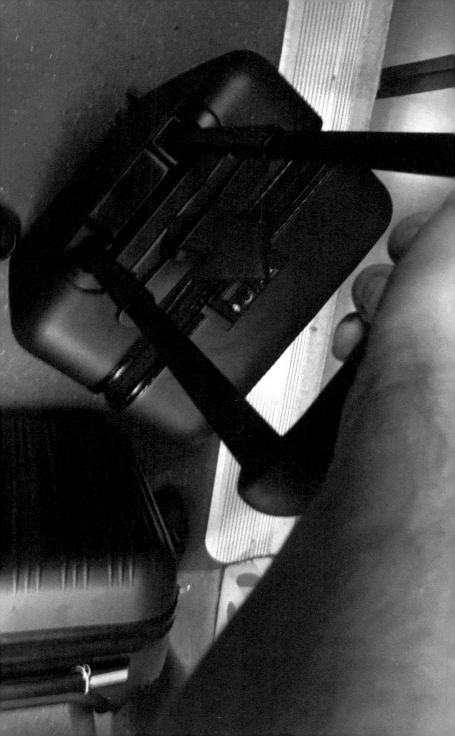

I. PACK LIGHT FOR LONDON

By far, the worst part of traveling to Britain is dealing with luggage. It's heavy and hard to get through airports, the Tube, and around London's bumpy sidewalks. Now that airlines charge extra for heavier luggage and extra bags, it's just not worth the added cost and trouble.

Our travel philosophy is that less is more when it comes to packing for London.

You don't need to take as much with you as you think. London hotels are small, and there won't be much room for massive luggage. Redefine what you think is essential when traveling and try to keep everything down to one carry-on and one checked bag. In recent years, we've dispensed with the checked bag altogether. We buy the biggest regulation carry-on bag, and then take only a carry-on with us (one for each of us). We've found carry-on only travel to be liberating. We move through the airport so much faster, and you don't have to worry about your bag getting lost (which has happened to us more than once). Inevitably, you'll come home with more things than when you arrived, so we recommend a cheap collapsible duffle or something similar. Check that on the way home.

Pack simply, plan your outfits in advance, be willing to mix and match. Try to keep shoes to a minimum. We usually take one pair of good walking shoes and a pair of dressier shoes.

If you want to pack really light, don't be afraid to do a load of laundry during your trip. Most hotels have facilities, and most neighborhoods have a laundromat. It's a great way to meet some locals. If you stay in self-catering accommodation, you'll usually have your own washing facilities.

2. YOU CAN BUY IT THERE!

It's tempting to think that you need to bring everything with you along with the kitchen sink. London is in a foreign country, and you absolutely need the specific haircare or skincare products you rely on. But you can buy pretty much anything in London that you can buy in a drugstore back home. Plus, it's a lot of fun to go into a British Boots or Superdrug and explore the miles of shelves to get some new toiletries.

Once, when our bags were lost, we had to go out and buy essentials like a change of clothes or two and some toiletries, and it is one of our favorite London memories. Now, when I pack for trips to London, I think really long and hard about whether I really need it all, and if I do, can I just get it there? If you travel with a carry-on only, this is the easiest way to get around TSA liquid regulations.

You may also discover wonderful new products that you'll end up using instead. My favorite soap, for example, comes from the Muji store on Long Acre in Covent Garden. Every time I'm in London I stock up and buy loads!

ONLY

RRP

£2

Tropicana.

PURE PREMIUM

SMOOTH

ORANGE WITH NO BITS

100% PURE SQUEEZED FRUIT

3. GROCERIES & SNACKING

Every neighborhood in London has a corner shop, a grocery store or, if it sells alcohol, an off-license or 'offy' for short. So if you want to save a ton of money eating, then we recommend stopping in on your first day in London.

Going to a grocery store and stocking up on snacks will save you a lot of money on meals, especially if you plan picnics. It's a great way to save money on food, which will be your highest cost while in London after lodging. You get the fun bonus of browsing the shelves in a British grocery store and seeing what the British like to eat and try some new things yourself.

If you have self-catering accommodation and can cook for yourself, stores like Marks & Spencer have daily deals where you can get an entire meal for two for just £10, including entree, dessert, and wine. It's a great deal for tasty food. You'll pay more at stores like Harrods, Waitrose, etc.

Breakfast is the most important meal of the day, so we always stock up on foods like muffins, fruits, and cereal. That way, we get a good breakfast in the room and, when we leave the hotel, we're fueled up for a full day of London sightseeing.

It's also nice to have healthy snacks on hand; sightseeing makes you hungry, and when it's 9 o'clock at night and you're exhausted and hungry, a bag of grapes or an apple goes a long way to staying healthy while you're traveling.

4. DEALING WITH THE RAIN

Despite the popular myth, it doesn't rain ALL the time in London. In fact, most of the year, London has pretty fair weather. Believe it or not, in 2012, London was under drought conditions! However, it COULD rain at any time, so carry a small umbrella with you. I purchased a nice travel umbrella online, it collapses into a very small package and fits into my carry-on. I'm always ready for rain when I travel to London. Carrying an umbrella won't look stupid, you look prepared. Bit of warning - if you ever do buy a really nice umbrella - be prepared to ship it home if it doesn't fit in your luggage, they won't let you take it through the security checkpoint. We learned this the hard way and once had to CHECK an umbrella. That had to be weird to load onto the plane!

5. CLOCKS & 24-HOUR TIME

Like the rest of Europe, the British use the 24-hour clock (aka military time) and the 12-hour clock interchangeably. Often you'll find TV and theatre showtimes quoted in 12-hour time, while trains and bus schedules will be in 24-hour time. This inevitably leads to confusion amongst travelers in London.

The solution is simple. The easiest way to translate the different clocks is this: subtract 12 from whatever the 24-hour time is. For example 23:00 = 11:00pm.

Another handy tip for dealing with this is to switch your phone to 24-hour time when you arrive in London; then, you can acclimate to it.

The old adage of 'measure twice, cut once' can definitely be adapted to London travel 'check the time twice, book once.'

LHR
LONDON, ENGLAND

6. CURRENCY & CARDS

Before traveling to London, we recommend getting a credit or debit card that does not have foreign transaction fees. There are plenty out there - the British Airways Chase Visa comes to mind immediately. My business bank card has foreign transaction fees, and these can add up to a sizable amount of money when we're traveling. Also, warn your bank that you'll be traveling.

After dragging their feet for what seemed like forever, American banks are finally moving their credit cards to chip & pin, which has been the standard in Britain for a long time. Though most cards are actually 'chip & sign,' which will irritate checkout staff as they always struggle to find a pen. But you no longer have to swipe your card, which makes things much smoother. The British have adopted contactless cards as well, and American banks have adopted those much faster. You can easily tap your card in Britain these days, and that's it.

You can buy British money here in the USA from various sources, but honestly, in this day and age, just wait until you get there and get it out of the ATM. ATMs give you that day's exchange rate, and most banks won't charge a fee for it. Though after years of travel, we have a small kitty of British money we take with us on every trip.

The British are very proud of their currency, the pound sterling. And now that Britain is leaving the EU at the end of this year, 2020, they will never adopt the Euro. The bills have changed in recent years. They're no longer made of paper but plastic. The bills in Scotland and Northern Ireland look different (and you may struggle to use them in England).

Many stores will also process the credit card transaction in dollars these days, but keep in mind that this is just another way for the store to make more money, and you're not guaranteed to get the best exchange rate by doing this. When in doubt, pay in pounds, whether you pay in cash or swipe.

In recent years, we've relied on the Transferwise service for our British money travel needs. Open to Americans, you can sign up for a free account, then carry a bank balance in British pounds. They also provide you with a chip & pin debit card that you can use while you're traveling in Britain. This makes it ridiculously easy as you pay for things like a local. On our next trip, we'll just load all our spending money on it and use that for expenses and to get cash out of the ATM. You'll save loads on fees and checkout staff won't get annoyed when they have to find a pen.

7. POWER SOURCES

We made the mistake of splashing out on an expensive voltage converter on one of our first trips to London. We never used it. You generally don't need a voltage converter, though, just a plug adapter. Most American appliances and electronics convert voltage on their own.

You can pick up plug converters pretty cheaply at most stores like Target or Walmart. Many come with a kit that has many. It's best to have 3 or 4 with you so you won't have to ration your electronic device charging.

Most computer chargers work fine in the UK. We use Apple products, and they make a plug adapter kit that has the UK adapter. If you use Apple products, then it's definitely worth picking up. It will work with all of them, and it only costs $40.

Keeping your phone charged is a critical task on any trip these days. USB chargers are a common standard all over the world. Do yourself a favor, go into a Pound Shop (like a dollar store), they're everywhere, and buy a £1 USB plug adapter. Then you have a way to charge your phone on British plugs and don't need to worry about getting an adapter that converts voltage. I have a few now, and they're handy on every trip now since USB charges so many things.

If you want to level up, buy a British power strip that you can carry with you. Then you have all the adapters and plugs you need to keep your gear charged. Most people don't have much 'gear' when they travel - but we do as every trip is a research trip - we have computers, cameras, phones, microphones, etc. that have to be charged.

The UK uses a higher voltage than American plugs - it's twice what American outlets are. This means they're DANGEROUS, which is why every plug has a switch. Don't forget to switch it on when you're charging something. I can't tell you how many times I've left my computer on the charger only to return to the hotel later to find it dead because I forgot to flip the switch. Also, because of the high voltage, you will NEVER find a plug in a British bathroom. The British are firmly in the water and electricity shouldn't meet camp.

If you need a curling iron or hairdryer - we highly recommend picking up a cheap one when you get to the country that's designed to work with the voltage. They take up too much space in your luggage! It will work better, anyway. If not, a plug adapter will usually suffice.

8. TRADING HOURS

Britain is not quite a 24-hour society like the USA. This is slowly changing, but you will be very surprised to see when things actually close. Many places in London are closed on Sundays or have different operating hours, including museums and stores.

Retail stores are usually open for only 6 hours on Sundays (10 am to 4 pm typically), so it's important to check ahead before setting out. The British government has begun to change this, but many stores still stick to the old Horus. You really can't rely on a store to always be open. We once planned to go to Harrods on the last Sunday on one of our trips. We went all the way there to find that the doors were locked because they were closed on Sundays. We missed our chance as we had a flight to catch. Harrods is now open on Sundays, but it's always a good idea to check operating hours before heading to a destination. If there is a specific store or place you want to visit, always double-check its opening hours to make sure you can.

Most stores adopt limited trading hours on Public Holidays, also known as Bank Holidays, which change every year. Always a good idea to check with the UK government website gov.uk and search for Public Holidays and make sure you don't book a trip then. Why? These are the days the British are off work and holidaying, so tourist attractions will be particularly packed, especially the free ones.

9. ALWAYS PACK A JACKET

I once went to England in July (well actually I've been in July several times). The first part of my trip were typical hot summer days like you would find in North America, and I had packed accordingly. Then, a weather system moved in. The temperature dropped into the 40s (Fahrenheit), and it rained. I had not packed a jacket. I froze at an outdoor concert.

So, what lesson did we learn, class?

Always pack a bloody jacket, so matter what time of year you're going. In fact, since a jacket takes up room in a carry-on suitcase, wear the jacket in the airport and on the plane (they're always cold anyway).

Make sure the jacket is relatively warm, it can get cold suddenly in Britain, even in July. If you want to be doubly prepared, make sure it's slightly waterproof.

You won't regret bringing the jacket.

But you will regret not bringing one (good jackets are expensive in Britain!).

10. AVOID HALF-TERM TIME

More than likely, you've never heard the term 'half-term.' But the British live for half-term.

Half-term is the break in the middle of school terms, usually a week-long, that the kids have off school. The British school year is divided into three terms. Each term has a break in the middle. Think of it like three spring-breaks (except they're all throughout the year).

In Britain, school is very strict; parents are simply not allowed to pull kids out of school to go on a holiday. And they can only be pulled out of school for deaths in the family or other awful circumstances. Parents get fined for taking their kids out of school if it's not authorized.

So, as a consequence, the British domestic tourist industry is scheduled around half-term. This is when Brits go on holiday. When they visit their museums. When they visit their stately homes and other attractions. Especially the free ones (the British are a very frugal people). We once tried to visit the Natural History Museum in London and didn't know it was half-term. The museum is free and the line was literally a mile long.

If you're booking self-catering accommodation, or a rental car, or a hotel, you will find that the prices are usually higher during half-term time. They can charge more during half-term (even if it's craven price gouging) because they are likely to have more bookings then. Consequently, you can usually get a great deal when it's not half-term.

If you're coming from across the ocean for a trip to Britain, avoid half-terms. The dates change every year, but you can always check the UK government website at gov.uk so you can plan accordingly.

11. STAYING CONNECTED

Staying connected while traveling in London is more important than ever. And your smartphone is now the most important guidebook when traveling. When we first started visiting London in the early 2000s, smartphones weren't even a thing. We had to carry guidebooks and maps with us (which I actually kind of miss). Nowadays, your phone is indispensable while in London. But this creates another problem: roaming charges.

We've all used our shiny smartphone in London with no problem, only to get home and get a surprise bill for hundreds and hundreds of dollars because we didn't know how much it would cost. So, it's important to check your carrier's international roaming policy before you leave for London.

Most will have an option for when you're traveling. For example, we use AT&T for our phones. They provide a simple international roaming package. It's $10 a day for unlimited data, text and call roaming per phone. It's well worth it. Key point, though, you have to sign up for this advance. If you don't...

There are services that will let you rent a smartphone while in London but really, since most of us have smartphones, this is simply not necessary, and it can be very expensive. At one time, I used to have a UK smartphone and phone number. But it was never really that useful; it was always easier to just use my US phone. If you have a spare smartphone (by this point, we all have old phones sitting in drawers) and it's unlocked, you could always get a SIM in the UK and have it activated again.

But again, this is usually more trouble than it's worth. Just take your US smartphone, make sure it's compatible with the UK networks (3G or 4G LTE - CDMA won't work in the UK). Pay the roaming charges. It makes things a lot easier. There's also free WiFi everywhere. You'll have free WiFi in the hotel, in attractions, in restaurants, all over London streets. Your carrier may also provide access to UK wide WiFi (like AT&T does). Staying connected is easy, just make sure you opt into a roaming package before you leave.

One final tip. Some airlines provide cell phone service on the plane (I'm looking at you Aer Lingus). This may seem convenient, but these airplane networks are not usually covered by US Carrier Roaming Packages. I got a rude $160 wake-up when I accidentally turned my phone on during a transatlantic flight.

Tired of London, Tired of Life   TOM JONES

Virgin BOOKS

LONDON

BLUE
GUIDE

SECRET LONDON   ANDREW DUNCAN

NH
NEW
HOLLAND

LONDON

Rick Steves'
LONDON   2012

AVALON
TRAVEL

12. TOP 5 LONDON GUIDEBOOKS

While the iPhone is a great tool for planning your trip to London, there's still nothing like opening the pages of a good guide book and planning your trip. Here's our selection of guide books worth owning.

1. **Rick Steves' London** - The standard-bearer for planning a trip to London, Rick's books are accessible, easy to read, and feature a ton of great information. Do not go to London without it.

2. **DK Eyewitness London** - This book is more useful for its treasure trove of pictures rather than up-to-date tourist information. But it serves a purpose in making London recognizable and putting key places on the map (something the Rick Steves' book shuns).

3. **Tired of London, Tired of Life by Tom A Jones** - A new guide book that features something new to do every day of the year. It's filled with unique experiences, many of which you wouldn't normally find in a London guide book.

4. **Secret London by Andrew Duncan** - This is not really a guide book, but more of a peek into the sites of London that tourists don't normally see. It features tons of interesting information as well as guided walks if you're an intrepid explorer.

5. **The Blue Guide to London - 18th Edition** - A guide to London for the intelligent, independent traveler, covering all the sights, contexts, dining, accommodations, and transportation with a focus on history, art, and architecture combined with excellent coverage of museums. They have a long pedigree - publishing since 1918. The most recent edition is a treasure.

13. FUN NIGHTS IN LONDON

Looking for some fun things to do on a night out in London? Often, we're so exhausted after a day of sightseeing that all we want to do is order in for dinner and watch British telly. But how often are you in London? If after a rest you can muster some more energy, here are a few ideas for things you can do. We've never been clubbers or bar types, so these are some fun things we've done in the evenings.

Leicester Square - The center of London's entertainment scene, there's plenty of places to eat, movie theatres, casinos, adult stores, and much more. Something for everyone.

See a Musical - You really can't go all the way to London without seeing a West End Musical. Les Mis is one of our favorites. Note that almost all theatres are closed on Sundays.

Go to the movies - A movie is a fun thing to do and won't break the bank. Try to see something you can't see back home. You don't go all the way to London to see a movie you can see at your local multiplex.

Eat a fancy dinner - Save a little of your budget to eat at some of London's nicer restaurants. There are plenty in Covent Garden and the area around there. Our favorite is Gordon Ramsay's Maze Grill on Grosvenor Square. Most expensive meal we ever had, but it was by far the best.

Walk along the Southbank - The Southbank (which means the southside of the Thames) is home to a vibrant arts and dining scene. You'll also enjoy great views of London lit up by night.

London Eye Night Flight - The London Eye at night is an amazing experience as you get to see the capital lit up in all its glory. Book ahead and, if you have the budget to spare, go for a champagne flight.

Classical Music Concerts - London is a center of classical music entertainment. No matter the time of year, there are always classical concerts on. By far, our favorites are going to the St Martin-in-the-Fields evening concerts. The acoustics are amazing, and it's a beautiful old church. Tickets are usually very inexpensive, and you can get an intermission drink in the crypt café below.

Museum Lates - A recent trend is museums extending opening hours into the evenings for special events and exhibitions. The museums are usually much less crowded, and you can enjoy the exhibits to yourself.

London Sky Garden - One of London's newer attractions, and it's free. The Sky Garden is perched at the top of 20 Fenchurch Street and has expansive views of all over London, and it's particularly lovely at night. They have several bars and ample seating so you can enjoy a drink and the views. There are also restaurants if you want to eat. And the gardens are a joy to walk around - it's amazing to be in a garden in the sky!

14. BEST LONDON APPS

Here is our selection of Smartphone apps that you can't live without when traveling to London; they're now an indispensable travel accessory.

TripAdvisor - Over the last few years, Expedia ate the travel industry, and now TripAdvisor is the default travel knowledge app for many people. It's free and is filled with useful info. It will tell you which places to avoid (attractions, food, hotels, etc.). The reviews can generally be trusted (however, always be skeptical of the really bad ones, it's not always the place's fault).

Google Maps - A good companion to TripAdvisor, Google Maps is a very useful app for finding places to eat and things to do while you're in London. It's also very good at giving turn-by-turn directions when you're on foot.

Visit London - The app put out by the official London Tourist Authority. It's pretty much the only app that gives you a database of events going on in London at any given time. It also has an attraction finder. It's free.

Gett/Uber/Addison Lee - You cannot travel to London now without having a smartphone app ready to pay for ride-hailing. Gett is the best app for getting a Black Taxi in London. We're not huge fans of Uber, but it can prove useful in London. Addison Lee is a 'posh' Uber and allows you to book private cars. We usually use Addison Lee to book our transport to the airport.

CityMapper - If you don't want to use Google Maps, we recommend Citymapper, which was created in London and where they perfected their technology. It's the ultimate London journey planner. It will give you directions on the Tube, buses, trains, cycles, walking, etc. It's free and easy to use.

Tube Map - The standard map for the London Underground also features a guide to each line, stations, a route planner, and it will also locate you with GPS and tell you the closest Tube station.

Central London A to Z - There are several A-Z apps for London, but the mini one is suitable for tourists and features a map of central London with all the major attractions. It works offline and also uses GPS to locate you to help guide you on your way. It's also fun to look at.

15. TOP 5 NOTTING HILL

Notting Hill has been made famous by the film of the same name, which has been a blessing and a curse for the area. Notting Hill has become an American colony of sorts as many American ex-pats who moved to London to work in Britain's banking sector settled here. Here's our list of five things to do in the neighborhood, which is still charming even if most could never afford to live there.

1. **The Market** - While it's very crowded on Saturdays, definitely pay a visit to the Portobello Road Market. Get there early if you want to avoid the crowds. If you want a feeling of 'real' London, follow the market to past the West Way overpass, and you'll see some more local color with fruit & veg vendors and a more flea market feel.
2. **Hummingbird Bakery** – American-style baked treats that are better than you can get back home. We can also highly recommend their baking cookbook.
3. **Eat a Meal** - Notting Hill has a world-class selection of restaurants. Though the main streets have been taken over by the high-street chains, there are still tons of fun restaurants on the side streets.
4. **Museum of Brands, Packaging, and Advertising** - A neat little niche museum on an interesting topic. Britain's only museum dedicated to the art & design behind advertising. The focus is on British advertising, so you get an interesting perspective. They recently moved to a bigger location.
5. **The Blue Door** - Those who've seen the movie Notting Hill will certainly want to visit this iconic location that marked the entrance to Hugh Grant's flat. 280 Westbourne Park Road is the physical location of the door, which naturally became very popular after the film was released. Also, pay a visit to the Notting Hill Bookshop, which used to be called the Travel Bookshop and the one the movie was based on.

16. TIPPING IN LONDON

This is a complicated topic, but we'll try to address it as simply as possible. Generally, you don't need to tip in London. Whereas in America tipping is the default for pretty much everything, that is not the case in London. The reason for this is that tipping culture is a uniquely American thing rooted in the way it pays service staff. The UK doesn't have this simply because most service staff are paid a living wage and do not need tips to top up their income. That being said, there are still situations where tipping happens (why that is, is beyond the scope of this tip!).

First, in a restaurant, you usually don't have to tip. This is because most restaurants have a service charge tacked onto the bill that is essentially a mandatory tip that's paid to service staff. However, if there isn't a service charge, then it's acceptable to tip 10%. Tipping in a pub is unusual as most don't have table service. If, perhaps, it's a 'gastropub' that serves food, then treat tipping as you would in a restaurant.

Services are a little different. In a Black London Cab, for example, it's a common courtesy to round up to the next pound when paying. If you receive some other sort of service and are happy with it, then no one will be unhappy with a tip, but most service workers will treat it as unexpected (and usually be surprised).

When staying in hotels, most staff do not expect tips in any way. In higher-end hotels, it's acceptable to tip a few pounds to the bell-hop, but generally, you don't have to pay tips in hotels. It's also not common to tip your housekeeper.

One of the trends in London is offering free tours. The catch is that at the end of the 'free' tour, you're often expected to tip the tour guide. This is fine, if you're on a free tour and enjoyed yourself, then tip the guide. If, however, you've paid for the tour, you do not need to tip.

You may be thinking; surely, anyone will be happy to get a few extra pounds for a job well done? And you may well be right. But as tipping is perceived differently in Britain, it comes off more as 'rich Americans who don't know any better throwing their money around' than 'I'm getting extra for a job well done.'

It's a fine line between what's expected of you as a tourist and what's acceptable to you in your human interactions. But don't ever feel obligated to tip if you receive bad service. This is usually a moral argument in America; if you don't tip someone even when the service was bad, they don't get paid at all. In Britain, if you get bad service and don't tip, they still get paid.

17. STAND ON THE RIGHT!

This may seem counter-intuitive in a country famed for driving on the left side of the road. But in most situations in Britain, when you're walking, you walk on the right. If you're standing on an escalator, you stand on the right.

This may seem a minor concern, but on escalators and similar situations, this is so people who are in more of a hurry than you can get around you. This is most noticeable on the Tube. There the escalators are wide enough for two people to pass each other. If you stand on the left, people will bump into you or ask you to move. Don't worry, there are signs to remind you. Pay attention, so no one runs into you or is forced to say "'scuse me, love."

This is a huge source of frustration for Londoners as they navigate tourists on the network. This rule works for sidewalks as well - just try to stay out of the way. Also, when you stand on an escalator with your luggage, do not put your luggage next to you, blocking the 'fast lane' to your left. Put your luggage in front of you, so the patch is clear. If your luggage is so big that it will block the way either way, then consider the elevator or holding it sideways on the escalator.

London is a place that people live and work in, we're just visitors. Show them some courtesy by trying to stay out of their way.

18. LOOK RIGHT! AND LEFT!

Traffic in Britain generally comes from the right - not the left as it does in the USA. It's important to remember this when crossing any street.

Really, you should always look both ways, but it's important to train your mind to check the right. There are also a lot of one-way streets in London where you would do well to look left.

If you forget, generally there will be writing on the street crossings that tell you to look right, but you can't always rely on this.

On major streets there are usually controlled crosswalks that safely control the flow of traffic and people. On less busy streets there aren't, so when you cross the street you have to be very careful, cabbies and locals drive FAST on local roads. You do not want to end up in the emergency room (A&E).

19. QUEUE UP OR ELSE!

I t is often joked that queuing up (or 'standing in line' to the rest of us) is a cherished national pastime in Britain. They do take it very seriously.

In the USA when there's a line for something, unless directed by a higher authority, there will be chaos as people cut in and attempt to get to the front first. In Britain, the British line up automatically without direction and maintain the integrity of the line (no cutting! Or queue jumping as they call it).

Queuing creates situations where you'll have time to chat with Brits. It's a good way to make a "line friend," but don't expect it to go beyond that. Safe topics to talk about include the weather, the weather, and the weather.

You'll find queues in the most unexpected places. And their organization will be ironclad. Once when getting off a transatlantic flight, we needed a taxi. At Paddington Station, we followed a line on the ground all the way to the taxi rank. Only to find a very long line of people waiting for their turn. This struck us as odd - can't you just shout 'Taxi!'?!? Nope, you stand in line and wait. Bleary-eyed and jetlagged makes this fun!

As an American, you'll just have to learn to stand in line and be patient about it. It bears repeating: do not, under any circumstance, jump the queue. Brits hold a grudge for life.

20. A GUIDE TO LONDON PUBS

The pub is at the center of British cultural life, and you would be remiss to skip it on a trip to London. Most neighborhoods have a pub that's a good place to relax, meet locals, maybe get a good meal, and become a temporary local.

Here are a few tips, so you don't look like a pillock (that's an idiot in American speak).

1. You go to the bar to order food and drinks. Not all pubs serve food. Sometimes the best you can hope for is a packet of crisps. In a traditional pub, there is no table service. If they serve food, you get a table number, and the food is brought to you.

2. In Britain, you order beer by the pint or half-pint. A pub will have plenty of other drink options like wine, soft drinks, tea, coffee, water, etc.

3. There is generally no tipping in a British pub unless it's a gastropub, then restaurant tipping rules apply.

4. Don't be horrified if you see a child or a dog in a pub; this is normal in Britain.

5. If you go with a group, it's common for each person in the group to take orders and buy a round of drinks. They take this very seriously, do not expect to drink for free - everyone takes a turn. And do not leave before it's your turn.

6. The legal drinking age in Britain is 16 if you're with an adult, and 18 if you're on your own.

21. LONDONERS ARE NOT LIKE AMERICANS

Londoners are not like Americans – they are a breed unto themselves. You wouldn't expect a Londoner to be like someone from your local town, would you?

They do things differently – sometimes VERY differently. This will seem alien to you, but it's very normal for them.

You're there to learn, observe, and enjoy yourself (never to judge). The sooner you lose the expectation that a Londoner will treat you like a fellow American would, the sooner you'll enjoy your trip.

Londoners do not look like you may expect them to. Popular culture paints a picture of pasty white people with bad teeth. London is a very diverse place, and most people's teeth are fine now.

What binds all Londoners together is a shared identity that they're all Londoners. And anyone can become a Londoner if they've been there long enough.

22. AVOID CHUGGERS

A chugger is someone you won't be able to avoid on London's streets – especially in busy tourist areas. Slang for "charity muggers," they're people who work on commission for charities.

They accost you on the sidewalk and ask you to donate to their cause. While this sounds rather nice, they actually pocket a percentage as their earnings.

They are annoying and can be very aggressive as they are trying to make some money by you supporting a good cause. You will not offend them by ignoring them or telling them to bugger off.

If, however, you come across a 'Big Issue' seller, they are not chuggers and are, in fact, very respected. The Big Issue is a magazine published for the benefit of homeless people or those in need. They get to keep the money they make when they sell their magazines, and the publishers help them get their lives sorted out. It's a fantastic cause - and the quality of the articles in it is pretty good.

23. DON'T BRING UP THE WAR

This may seem like common sense to most, but don't ever bring up World War II in casual conversation. It's a political minefield.

The British are extremely proud of their wartime history and, contrary to the popular myth, they suffered a great deal and for quite a bit longer until we bothered to get involved (and will not hesitate to mention this to you).

We did not "save their asses in the war," so don't even think of saying that. If you think this never happens, it does. We've seen it ourselves.

24. THE CUSTOMER IS NOT ALWAYS RIGHT

The British have a far different conception of customer service than the USA. Always be prepared for poor customer service – especially on the railroads. While most Americans default to verbally assaulting ineffective customer service, avoid doing it in Britain. It will get you nowhere.

Expect poor customer service everywhere, and when you get GOOD customer service, it will come off as a bit of a treat. Service is the worst in London's restaurants – even in the nice ones. If you have low expectations, you'll be delighted when you get decent customer service (and then have something to talk about with your British friends as they love to complain and gossip about the service they've received).

25. LONDON IS VERY DIVERSE

London is an incredibly diverse city, and it has been throughout its history. It's absorbed immigrants from all over the world and the former British Empire, all of which have contributed to London's unique identity as a truly global city. It's been said that hundreds of languages are spoken in London, united by a common one - English.

You will come across many different types of people on your London trip and, if you come from a predominantly monocultural area in America, this can be disorienting.

But all of these cultures have created the London that we know and love. Whether it's the French Huguenots who brought European ideals to Britain or Jewish pogrom refugees who brought to Britain its most famous dish: fish & chips. Or immigrants from the Caribbean who brought Britain a rich musical and cultural heritage after World War II. Or South Asian immigrants who came home when they were expelled from Uganda and found themselves running Britain's corner shops. All of these peoples create a rich tapestry that is modern London.

London is a truly global city, and it's possible to get through the whole day without actually encountering any Brits at all. Because of this, many people perceive London to be a rather rude city because it's full of foreigners. It is. Be prepared for it. Most restaurants have foreign waiters and waitresses, and it can be hard to communicate, but you'll just have to get used to it. Be kind and patient.

26. THE SPECIAL RELATIONSHIP

Don't expect special treatment because you're an American or because we "saved them in the war." To the British, you're just like every other foreign visitor— you're just more cheerful, louder, and speak a similar language (and they argue we ruined THEIR language).

The biggest wakeup call you'll get when you leave the US for the first time is when you have to get in line at Heathrow for Customs with everyone else in the world, while the British sail through the Citizen line. As Americans, we have no special rights in the UK other than we can travel there for up to 6 months without a visa.

In Britain's legal system you have the same rights as any other foreigner - and British person - for that matter. You can still get pulled over for speeding, and you will absolutely have to pay the fines. You'll also find that most problems that Americans run into while traveling can be fixed if you know the right people.

27. PRONUNCIATION GUIDE

Many of London's famous places are not pronounced the way you think they are or the way you'd assume from how they're spelled. Here's a list of London places with unusual pronunciations. Most locals will be quite chuffed if you can say these correctly!

- Aldwych - 'Old witch'
- Borough - 'Burra' not 'burrow'
- Cadogan Square - KA-duggan, not KAD-ogen (see film Notting Hill)
- Chiswick - 'Chiz-ick' - the w is silent
- Clapham - Clap-em not Clap-ham.
- Deptford - Debt-ford - the p is silent
- Dulwich - Dull-itch - the w is silent
- Greenwich - Gren-itch - the w is silent
- Grosvenor Square - Grove-Ner - the s is invisible
- Hainault - Ay-nolt - the h is silent
- Holborn - Ho-burn - the l is silent
- Homerton - Ommer-ton - the h is silent
- Leicester Square - Lester, not Lie-ces-ter.
- Marylebone - Marly-bone (as in Jacob Marly)
- The Mall - The Mal - not mall as in the place (or Darth Maul)
- Pall Mall - This one is a tongue twister challenge - Pal Mal - Pal as in friend and Mal as in Mal.
- Penge - This one rhymes with Henge.
- Rotherhithe - Rother-hive
- Ruislip - Rye-slip
- Southwark - Suth-uk - this one is hard - google it!
- Streatham - Stret-em
- Theydon Bois - They-Don-Boyce
- Tottenham - Tott-Num
- Wapping - Similar to shopping not rapping
- Woolwich - Wool-idge not 'wool witch'

28. QUIET DOWN!

When Londoners were recently surveyed about American tourists, the top annoyance on their list of complaints was that Americans are LOUD.

While it may be hard for Americans to stomach, we are indeed very loud, especially when we're traveling abroad. This may come as a surprise to you. But Americans are a loud and boisterous people, and it drives Brits mad when we're loud in their quiet, sedate country.

The British are a quiet and reserved people (almost to a fault). And while they'll give you the benefit of the doubt if you speak too loudly (you don't know any better), try to bring your voice down a few notches while you're in London. Don't worry, people will still be able to hear you.

You will have to train your hearing when conversing with Brits. In busy places, it can sometimes be difficult to have a conversation because they speak too quietly. But the quietness is for the greater good of everyone else there.

We once had Sunday roast in a London pub, which was generally pretty quiet. We were having a nice, quiet chat with our British friends (we have learned to speak more quietly!). Then a group of Americans sat down next to us, and the volume in the already crowded room was substantially increased. We were slightly embarrassed.

Speak softly. Please.

29. LONDON'S FREE NEWSPAPERS

ondon's workers are a captive audience in the commuting hours, and there are a lot of them - more people commute into central London for work than actually live there. So, there are several free newspapers to cater to their tastes. Most of them are pretty good.

My favorite, by far, is The Evening Standard, which used to not be free, but is now. Handed out at all London Tube stations, it's basically London's local newspaper, and I love picking it up to get an idea of what Londoners are concerned about. Uniquely, the Evening Standard is printed in the afternoons and handed out at the evening rush hour (thus the name!). It will usually have that day's news! It's one of the last evening papers in the world.

Metro is a free paper put out by The Daily Mail (hiss). It's a more conversational newspaper and, while the Standard will usually make it home with most people, the Metro will usually be carpeting Tube trains by the end of the day.

City A.M. is a more high-brow free newspaper targeted at the busy London commuters going to work in the 'City of London' - usually in the financial industry.

30. LONDON FILMS & TV SHOWS

Many of us grew up with London films and TV shows as our escape to this great city. So, here's a handy list of London films and TV shows you can watch to get 'London Ready.'

London Films:

- Notting Hill
- Closer
- Match Point
- Sliding Doors
- Run Fatboy Run
- Passport to Pimlico
- About Time
- About a Boy
- One Day
- Love Actually
- Long Good Friday
- Paddington 1 & 2

London Set TV Shows:

- Absolutely Fabulous
- Peep Show
- The IT Crowd
- Eastenders
- 2012/W1A
- The Thick of It
- Ashes to Ashes
- Black Books
- Call the Midwife
- The Crown
- House of Cards (BBC)
- Jeeves & Wooster
- Law & Order UK
- Lead Balloon
- Luther
- NY-LON
- Only Fools & Horses
- Sherlock

31. TOP FIVE WEST END

London's West End area is its most vibrant and tourist friendly. Here's our list of five things you should do when you're in the area.

1. **Take in a show** - Les Mis is one of our favorites, though not very British in subject matter!
2. **Stroll through Covent Garden** - Lots of wonderful shops and a beautiful piazza.
3. **Eat a Meal in Leicester Square** - Plenty of tourist-themed fine dining in the area.
4. **Visit the National Gallery and people-watch in Trafalgar Square** – World-class art in a beautiful setting plus the best place to watch people in London.
5. **Cecil Court Stroll** - While London's famous book district along Charing Cross Road is mostly gone, Cecil Court is still going strong with several second hand and antiquarian bookshops.

32. TOP 5 KNIGHTSBRIDGE

K nightsbridge has a reputation as a very wealthy area, but it's also filled with many culturally rich attractions. Here's our selection of five things you can do in the area.

1. **Harrods** - You cannot go to London without going there.
2. **Hyde Park and Kensington Gardens** - Our favorite London park has so much to see and do.
3. **Victoria & Albert Museum** - An eclectic mix of many subjects in British design in a beautiful setting.
4. **Natural History Museum** - Dedicated to Natural History, next to the Science Museum - don't miss the Darwin Centre.
5. **Royal Albert Hall** - Considered the national performing arts venue, take in a concert in this beautiful Victorian building in the area of London whose development was spearheaded by Prince Albert.

33. GET A HOTEL CLOSE TO THE TUBE

You will likely be spending a lot of time on the Tube as it's the easiest and cheapest way to get around Central London. Make sure that you don't spend a lot of time walking to the nearest Tube Station. It's no big deal in the morning when you're ready to see London, but at the end of the day, it can feel like a slog if your hotel is far from the Tube.

When booking your hotel, check Google Maps and make sure it's near a Tube station. Most hotel websites show how close they are, but be careful — many just say the distance, but that doesn't mean anything on London's spaghetti streets. There's nothing worse than a 1-mile walk going in circles on London's confusing streets at the end of the day when you're exhausted from seeing the sites.

34. IS IT HOT IN HERE?

Despite London being a modern 'First World' country, you will be surprised to find that most hotels and businesses don't have air conditioning. This is hard to get used to in London.

Generally, you don't need air conditioning, because London stays moderately cool most of the year. There are a couple of months in the summer, though, where things get really hot, especially on the Tube.

It's not so much that it gets sweltering – temperatures above 85 degrees Fahrenheit are pretty uncommon. It's just that you never have a chance to cool off, so it feels hotter than it actually is.

The Tube gets oppressively hot as most of it is not air-conditioned, the masses of people create an astounding amount of heat, and London's unique geology means that its clay has stored heat over the decades.

Carry a bottle of water with you, and try to avoid the Tube in July and August. Thankfully, most new hotels have air conditioning so, if your budget allows you to stay in one of them, you'll be able to cool off. Older and budget hotels, however, will usually not have air conditioning. Pro-tip: go to a local hardware store (called an Ironmonger) and buy a fan. You will not regret it. Actually, buy a fan no matter what time of year you're there. Trust me.

35. HOTEL ROOMS ARE SMALL

Unless you can afford to spend $500+ a night, your hotel room will be small and not up to the standards you'd expect from a Holiday Inn in America.

This is pretty much the way it is in London. Budget hotels feature small rooms, windows without a view (unless a concrete courtyard is a view), musty furnishings, and sometimes tiny TVs. Staff will generally be unhelpful (and Eastern European). They'll also be rather noisy (especially during the breakfast rush).

Don't be sold on a hotel based on "free continental breakfast." This will most likely be the food you won't want to eat, or all the good food will be gone before you get down there. It's usually a buffet featuring soggy eggs and toast. It's not worth paying extra for it. In the post-Covid-19 world, most hotels will likely dispense with breakfast buffets.

We're rather prosaic about hotels. We just think of it as a place to lay our heads at night. You don't need an excuse to stay in your room anyway. A crappy hotel gives you an excuse to spend as much time out in London as possible. But a very good hotel can enhance your stay in ways you don't expect.

You'll have a more familiar 'American' experience at newer hotels. But even here, you will find the rooms are much smaller than in the US.

36. HOTEL CHECK-IN TIME

Many of the flights from the USA land in the early London morning, some as early as 6 am. While this is kind of nice as you have the whole day ahead of you, it's usually not since you can't check into most hotels until after 3 pm in the afternoon.

Some will let you check in early, but more often than not, you'll be sitting around their lobby for a few hours waiting to check-in. If you're staying at a good hotel, you can check your bags with the concierge, and then go out and explore for the day before checking into your room at the proper time (but take your passport and valuables with you).

Also, many of the cheaper touristy hotels cater to package tours, and the busloads of tourists usually arrive right at check-in time, so get your place in line first, or else you'll find yourself in line with a bunch of grumpy Germans.

We recommend dropping off your bags and then eating a good breakfast/lunch – this will help reset your body clock. Higher-end hotels might allow you to book an early check-in or move things around so you can get into your room early. Tourist-class hotels won't really care. You'll just have to wait.

37. BEWARE OF BED BUGS

The creepy crawlies have made a comeback in London, and we've seen some real horror stories from our readers and friends.

If you're not familiar with bed bugs, they're bugs that live in mattresses. They like to come out at night and bite unsuspecting blood donors. Their bites irritate the skin, and often they're bad enough to require some sort of medical intervention.

Always check your mattress for bed bugs before settling in. They like to hide behind the mattress against the wall and in between the mattress, box spring, and the mattress seams. Don't be afraid to move things around and see.

If you spot a bedbug, immediately pick up your bags and get out of the room before they infest your bags, and you bring them home with you as they're very hard to get rid of.

This tip even goes for nice hotels. Cleaner, nicer hotels are not immune to the creepy crawlies! We also recommend checking TripAdvisor before you book to make sure there haven't been any bed bug attacks lately. Reviewers will often report this (with gruesome pictures).

38. FAMILY? TRY SELF-CATERING

Self-catering flats are a great way to live like a temporary local and experience living in London (something that's increasingly hard for Americans to do). However, renting a flat can be a little pricier than staying in a hotel.

If you're traveling in a group, renting a flat is the best option, as flats are well suited to families. You can get more than one bedroom for increased privacy and get full cooking facilities. You can save money on food by eating in.

We used to recommend London Connection, but they have since gone bust. Airbnb has pretty much swallowed the self-catering market in most major cities, so check there (we have never used it, however). We can, however, recommend HolidayLettings.co.uk, which is owned by Expedia, and we've had good experiences booking through them.

39.

TOP 5
ST. JAMES

St. James is a very genteel part of central London long associated with royalty and the upper classes. It's one of our favorite areas. Here are a few things you can do in the neighborhood.

1. **Fortnum & Mason** - An elegant department store famous for their hampers of British goods.
2. **Piccadilly Arcade** - A charming and old covered street featuring many fancy shops.
3. **St James's Palace** - It's not open to the public, but you can still admire its beauty and spot the odd British soldiers guarding its safety.
4. **Lock & Company Hatters** - One of the oldest hat makers in London with prices to match their pedigree.
5. **Green Park** - A stunning park not to be missed.

40. TOP 5 SOUTH KENSINGTON

South Kensington is one of our favorite areas in London (we've stayed there more than anywhere else). Here are our favorite things to do in the area.

1. **Kensington Palace** - The former home to Princess Diana recently went through a multi-million-pound renovation and is now the official London home of the Duke and Duchess of Cambridge.
2. **Holland Park** - A beautiful London park. One cool thing to do is take in a performance at the Open Air Theatre.
3. **Shop on Kensington High Street** - Find some of the world's most famous brands here.
4. **Leighton House Museum** - Stunning stately home that's recently been restored to its former glory.
5. **The Orangery** - Located near Kensington Palace, this stunning restaurant is perfect for High Tea.

41. FAMILIAR FOODS/ DIFFERENCES

The biggest shock to your system in London will be the differences in food. If you have sensitive digestion (like I do), your body will need time to adjust to those differences. While a meal may look or seem like the same thing you'd eat back home, it will be different. All food in Britain is slightly different.

Pancakes are more like crêpes than American pancakes.

They like to put crap in their hamburgers which makes them resemble meatloaf. They use different frying oils, so fried things have a different taste. Some things are even fried in beef dripping, no oil. Cuts of steak are similar. However, the fillet steak is usually the best cut you can find.

Burger King is better than McDonald's in the UK and tastes closer to home. Even if the food sounds familiar, always be prepared for it to taste different. Always read the menu carefully, and don't assume just because it has the same name that it's the same thing. Five Guys in London tastes exactly the same as it does back home in America.

42. CHAINS TO AVOID

Their food sucks and the service is generally horrible. We've not had many good experiences with the major chain restaurants (British and American).

Our stance is that you don't go all the way to Britain to have McDonald's, so why eat it?

The British chain restaurants are easy to spot in central London, as you'll see them all over the place. You can't spit without hitting a Garfunkel's or Aberdeen Steak House.

Look out for smaller cafes and mom and pop shops. They'll have the cheapest and tastiest food. Chain restaurants are geared toward tourists and have prices to match.

43. MCDONALD'S IS DIFFERENT

If you're looking for a respite from British cooking and think that you can relax with a Big Mac, keep in mind that it tastes completely different from how it does in the US. They use REAL beef in their burgers, and the oils they use on the fries are different, giving everything a strange - yet better - taste.

Also, their breakfast menu is a bit different than it is back home. I've searched in vain for hotcakes, but you'll never find them. One thing they do have (which the American ones should have) is donuts, which are rather tasty.

My favorite UK McDonald's meal are their crispy chicken strips and fries, something that is not on the menu in the USA. It's a quick and easy lunch on the go.

You also always have to ask for ketchup. It won't be out for you to help yourself.

44. PROPER FISH AND CHIPS

Proper fish and chips are comprised of one slab of battered fried fish (usually cod), a side of chips, often with mushy peas. You have never had authentic fish and chips outside Britain. Most places in America get it wrong and serve fried strips of fish. In reality, it's a slab of fish that's very challenging to eat with a knife and fork. Also of note is that the British eat with the fork tines DOWN when eating, and they don't switch hands as Americans do. In restaurants they're served properly with a tartare sauce, but no one will look down on you if you ask for ketchup. Chunky chips with fish are a highlight of any London trip. A late-night run to a chippy is a local London tradition, and you will find many places offering late-night treats of fish & chips. And if you don't like fish, you can get fried chicken and chips.

45. DON'T TRY TO BRING FOOD HOME

There's so much good food in London, but don't try to bring it home to the USA. We tried in the past, and it's almost always confiscated by US Customs and destroyed. The only foods that you can bring back into the USA are items that are packaged and sealed. Even then, Customs might give you a hard time.

When in doubt, ask if the store can ship to the USA. If they tell you they can't, you most likely won't be able to bring it home.

Ben's
Cookies

NO SMOKING.
It is against the law to
smoke in these premises

Ben's
Cookies

* Sorry this is the location in Oxford, it's the only picture of a Ben's Cookies I had!

46. THE BEST COOKIES!

We do love a nice cookie, and we highly recommend Ben's Cookies. They have a location in Covent Garden as well as several more around central London.

We highly recommend the double chocolate cookies. They're so good; it's the first place we go when we get off the plane!

Britain is known more for its biscuit culture than its cookie culture. Ben's is a bridge between the two - bringing massive American-style cookies to Britain. They're amazing.

© Hummingbird Bakery - Credit: Benjamin C. M. Backhouse

47. THE BEST CUPCAKES!

For the best cupcakes in the world, stop by the Hummingbird Bakery on Portobello Road in Notting Hill, which specializes in American-style baked goods. They have all kinds of baked goods, but their cupcakes are the best in London. So good, they've now got multiple locations all over central London and a bestselling cookbook!

48. TOP 5 ISLINGTON

Islington is a residential area popular with young Londoners, and the neighborhood has a great vibe to it. Here's our list of a few cool things to do in Islington.

1. **Football** - Take in a football match at Emirates Stadium.
2. **Le Mercury** - The best French food in the heart of London.
3. **Breakfast Club** - An 80s-themed breakfast joint that will feel like home to Americans, especially those from Chicago (John Hughes themed).
4. **Highbury Fields** - It's not Hyde Park, but this local park is green, open, and beautiful.
5. **Screen on the Green** - A beautiful old Art-Deco movie theater.

49. FREE MUSIC IN LONDON

London has many places where you can hear great music for free. Here's a list of five places. London street music is one of the joys of travel in London. You can hear it anywhere!

- St Martin in the Field's at lunchtime every day.
- Covent Garden Market on the lower levels.
- Buskers on the South Bank of the river.
- Southbank Centre - free music often.
- St James's Church in Piccadilly. Free music recitals at 1:10 pm on Mondays, Wednesdays, and Fridays.
- Buskers on the Tube (all over the network).

50. BUCKINGHAM PALACE OPENING

Buckingham Palace is one of the most popular tourist attractions in London, but most people don't know that it's generally only open to tours in August and September when the Queen is not in residence. When it opens, there's usually a special exhibition that you can see in addition to the State Rooms.

If you're in town during this time, it's well worth checking out. If you want to tour one of the Queen's other residences, check out Windsor Castle instead, which is a short train ride from central London. It has its own set of grand rooms, one of the most important art collections in the world, and it's open year-round. Windsor Castle even has its own changing of the guard.

51. CHANGING OF THE GUARD

The Changing of the Guard is one of the most popular must-sees on the tourist trail in London. It's worth seeing if you're interested in British ceremonial traditions (if you're not, don't bother).

The Changing of the Guard outside Buckingham Palace takes place daily throughout the summer months at 11:30 am. Outside the summer months, it takes place every other day.

Be sure to confirm by checking the Changing of the Guard website for precise dates.

Arrive about 30-60 minutes in advance so you can stake out a good spot near the fence. Otherwise, you'll be craning your neck. It's also fun to watch from the Victoria Memorial in the roundabout across the road from the palace.

Once you've seen it, though, you have seen it. It's not really something you need to see again!

52. TOURING THE HOUSES OF PARLIAMENT

Parliament is open to public tours, but the opening times vary. It's generally not open when Parliament is in session, except at weekends. When Parliament is not in session, it is usually open every day. For example, when Parliament has its summer recess, it'll be open most days.

You have to book tickets in advance through the official website at http://www.parliament.uk/visiting. On the tour, you'll get to see the House of Commons and Lords Chambers, the Queen's Robing Room, the Royal Gallery, and Westminster Hall.

Security is tight, and you're not allowed to take pictures except in Westminster Hall. Check ahead before planning on going. You also need to be prepared to go through airport-style security screening to get onto Parliament grounds.

I've done the tour, and it's fantastic - well worth going through the extra trouble to arrange it. Currently, you cannot tour Big Ben (Elizabeth Tower), but that may change in a few years when the renovations are complete (as of writing the clocktower was still covered in scaffolding).

15
St Paul's Cathedral
Fleet Street
Aldwych
TOWER HILL
42ND STREET
THEATRE ROYAL DRURY LANE
RM652
OPEN
WLT 652

53. CHEAP BUS TOUR OF CENTRAL LONDON

Most of the classic London double-decker Routemasters have been taken out of service, but they still run on one bus route in Central London: the Number 15. Since 2019, the heritage service operates only at weekends and on Bank or Public Holidays, from the last Saturday in March until the last weekend in September. Transport for London has hinted that they may withdraw this service eventually as well.

It's really affordable and fun to hop on, climb to the top, and ride the bus as it circles through all the London sites. It's also much less expensive than other bus "tours." You also get the bonus of riding an iconic piece of London heritage. If they're all withdrawn from service, ride on top on one of the 'new' double-decker buses, and you can get the same tour, and there will be aircon!

54. IS THE TATE MODERN WORTH A VISIT?

Well, you can never beat a free museum. While the building is very cool and worth a visit for that, the Tate Modern is very overrated unless you're really into modern art, which many people aren't. The gift shop is insanely expensive. I go just to admire the building and the massive Turbine Hall. The museum is free to enter, and they do have a few famous pieces of art, including some Monets and a Jackson Pollack. They've also recently extended the building with new galleries that are neat to look at. There's also a great restaurant at the top.

55. SPEAKERS' CORNER

This famous area in Hyde Park is considered the home of free speech where you are welcome to speak about anything you wish as long as you don't cause a riot. It's colorful, fun, and enlightening. You'll probably find speakers any day of the week, but Sunday is the best day to go. Some of the people speaking will be, shall we say, rather unconventional. It's like Twitter but in person.

56. TOP 5 LONDON PARKS

London has some of the most beautiful parks in the world, and they're definitely worth a visit. You can relax for free and enjoy a picnic while mingling with locals.

1. **Hyde Park/Kensington Gardens** - This is a must-visit. Check out the Serpentine Gallery, the paddle boats, the Princess Diana memorial, and much more. In the winter they usually have a Christmas carnival.
2. **Regent's Park** - A huge park to spend some time in, also home to the residence of the US Ambassador and London Zoo.
3. **St James's Park** - Don't miss the great views of Buckingham Palace from the bridge on the lake.
4. **Green Park** - Great place to have a rest under some beautiful trees.
5. **Hampstead Heath** - Don't miss the great views of the London skyline from Parliament Hill.

57. TOP 5 LONDON MUSICALS

You can't go to London without taking in a West End Show. Here are five classic shows that we recommend (and you should be able to get cheap tickets, too).

1. Wicked
2. Mamma Mia
3. Lion King
4. Les Misérables
5. Matilda

If musicals aren't your thing check out The Mousetrap, the world's longest-running play!

58. QUEENSWAY IS FUN

Queensway is not well known on the tourist track as it's primarily a residential area, but outside the Queensway Tube Station and north up the street are lots of interesting places to shop and eat. There are a lot of local places you won't find anywhere else.

The street contains many restaurants (particularly Chinese, Arab, and Mediterranean), pubs, letting agents, and high street stores. Near the northern end of the street is the former multistory Whiteleys Shopping Centre, on the site of London's first department store, opened by William Whiteley in 1867. It's now turned into flats, but the building is well worth looking at. There's also an interesting maze-like shopping mall that's reminiscent of a Middle Eastern souk. It's fun.

59. ST MARTIN IN THE FIELDS CONCERTS

This small church located just off Trafalgar Square is also a center for classical music in London. They have free concerts during the lunch period, and they have regular evening concerts – which are amazing – in the very old church that was recently renovated. The concerts are affordable as well, so if you're on a budget and want some culture, it's the way to go. During intermission, you can get a drink in the crypt café. After a concert, stroll through Trafalgar Square and then north to Leicester Square for a late dinner. It makes a perfect London night out.

60. 5 AMERICAN PLACES

You may come to London to see Britain, but there are a few bits of America in London that are a fun visit when you're in town.

1. Roosevelt Statue - Statue dedicated to Britain's wartime ally Franklin Roosevelt.

2. Franklin House - Ben Franklin's personal home during his time in London, recently restored to look exactly as it did when he lived there.

3. Ed's Easy Diner – American style-diner located near Victoria Station.

4. US Embassy - Recently opened, this state-of-the-art symbol of American power moved south of the river. It even has a moat! The 'old' embassy is still on Grosvenor Square, which has always been a center of American power in Britain. It's being turned into flats.

5. American Memorial Chapel at St Paul's - The American Memorial Chapel commemorates those Americans based in Britain who gave their lives in the Second World War.

61. RED PHONE BOXES

You'll see the iconic red phone box everywhere, but they're also getting harder to find as they have become completely redundant in the age of mobile phones. They are pretty easy to locate in the tourist areas, and many still work (but might smell like urine…).

It's always great fun to place a call home from one of them, and it's pretty convenient as you can swipe your credit card these days. Also, don't be surprised to see cards hanging in the phone booths for prostitutes. Some people collect them. But you may want to find a phone booth without them if your kids want a picture in a red phone box.

For the famous sculpture of a bunch of red phone boxes falling down, visit Old London Road in Kingston-Upon-Thames to see "Out of Order" by David Mach which was recently restored.

62. HOW TO SEE LONDON'S CATHEDRALS FOR FREE

Most cathedrals in London have a Choral Evensong service for the public to attend. It's a great way to hear some beautiful music in a stunning setting for free.

After they close the cathedrals to tourists, you can still go in and experience the nightly service, usually held around 5 pm, for free.

You won't be able to enjoy the touristy bits as they will be closed off, but you still get to experience the amazing spaces. It's respectful to remove your hat and put your camera away. If pictures are important to you, come during tourist hours though some restrict photography.

63. 6 UNKNOWN LONDON MUSEUMS

L ondon is home to a wide array of small museums that focus on some rather interesting subjects. Here's our selection of those worth a visit.

1. **The Cartoon Museum** - Dedicated to the art behind political cartoons and comics.
2. **Hunterian Museum** - Dedicated to animal specimens.
3. **The Fan Museum** - Dedicated to fans! The kind you wave to stay cool.
4. **Sir John Soane's Museum** - Dedicated to the history of design and architecture.
5. **Bank of England Museum** - Learn the history of money.
6. **Museum of Brands and Packaging in Notting Hill** - Dedicated to the history of advertising and branding.

PRIME
MERIDIAN
OF THE
WORLD

CENTRE OF TRANSIT CIRCLE
LATITUDE 51°28'38" NORTH
LONGITUDE 0°00'00"

EAST LONGITUDE	WEST LONGITUDE

Accurist

64. STRADDLE THE GLOBE

You can stand in two different hemispheres at the Prime Meridian located in the courtyard of the Royal Observatory in Greenwich.

Sadly, this attraction is no longer free, as you have to pay admission to the observatory. But the observatory is worth a visit on its own, so we highly recommend it.

If you don't want to stump up the money, you can see the meridian elsewhere in Greenwich Park!

65. THE BEST PEOPLE WATCHING

I f you want to just sit around and watch London go by, grab a sandwich, and sit on the steps to the National Gallery in Trafalgar Square for some of the finest people-watching in London. Though these days most of the people will be fellow tourists and performers (like the floating Yodas). If you want to see 'real' Londoners, check out Hyde Park or Hampstead Heath.

66. ZOO LIFE IN LONDON

There are two world-class zoos in London: The Battersea Park Children's Zoo and the ZSL London Zoo in Regent's Park. Perfect for kids and animal lovers!

67. MOVIE PREMIERES

The glitzy movie premieres in London always take place in Leicester Square. If you want to star watch, then grab a spot and wait for the show to begin! Be sure to arrive early as you can expect big crowds.

68. NATIONAL GALLERY

Dedicate at least half a day to exploring the National Gallery. It's still won't be enough, but give yourself time to explore the beautiful works of art. We definitely recommend going through with a guidebook or taking the audio tour.

Here's a quick list of 10 works of art you should try and see:

1. The Hay Wain by John Constable
2. Rain, Steam, and Speed by JMW Turner
3. The Fighting Temeraire by JMW Turner
4. Sunflowers by Van Gogh
5. Water Lily Pond by Monet
6. Mr and Mrs Andrews by Gainsborough
7. The Ambassadors by Holbein
8. The Arnolfini Portrait
9. Self-portrait by Rembrandt
10. Equestrian Portrait of Charles I

69. YOU CAN TOUR THE BBC

This has changed in recent years. The BBC offers tours of their newly renovated Broadcasting House in central London. The tour takes in the news studios, sets, and behind the scenes stuff. Book ahead as the tours are very popular. You get an excellent insight into how the BBC operates.

70. BEST FREE MUSEUMS IN LONDON

London is blessed with a world-class selection of museums with free admission. They often ask for donations, but you can still get in for free. Special exhibitions usually cost money to gain admission. The British love a bargain, so expect these museums to be crowded at weekends and during holidays. The following are some of our favourites:

- British Museum
- National Gallery
- National Portrait Gallery
- Tate Modern
- Tate Britain
- Museum of London
- Docklands Museum
- Natural History Museum
- Science Museum
- Victoria and Albert Museum
- Bank of London Museum
- Imperial War Museum
- London Political Cartoon Gallery
- National Maritime Museum
- Sir John Soane's Museum
- Temple of Mithras

71.

TOP 5
EAST END

The East End of London has a checkered reputation as a rough area, but that's changed quite a bit particularly since the 2012 Olympics. Here are our five things not to miss in the East End.

1. **Westfield Stratford City** - The largest shopping mall in Europe.
2. **Brick Lane Market** - A diverse and vibrant market not to miss!
3. **Museum of London's Docklands** - Explore London's maritime history at this free museum.
4. **The Geffrye Museum** - See how London families lived through the centuries.
5. **Whitechapel Gallery** - Wonderful art gallery.

ENGLAND

CALM
AND
CARRY
ON

£9.99

LONDON
and all I got
this LOUSY T-S

£7.99

NDON

ENGLAND

£9.99

KEEP
CALM
AND
SHOOT
ZOMBIES

My Sister
LONDE
and all I g
this LOUSY

£9.99

NDON

NGLAND

£9.99

KEEP
CALM
AND
CARRY
ON

My Dad went
LONDO
and all I got wa
this LOUSY T-Shir

ONDON

ENGLAND

£9.99

KEEP
CALM
AND
CARRY
ON

My Daughter went to
LONDON
and all I got was
this LOUSY T-Shirt!

72. ON BUYING SOUVENIRS

We understand the urge – the urge to snap up as many London-themed gifts as you can carry for everyone back home, especially if this is your first trip to London. There will not be a shortage of souvenir shops to tempt you into parting with your cash.

Pretty much every souvenir store in central London has all the same tatty crap. Most of it is made in China (not in Britain). Most of it is not that special. It's also been discovered that many central London tourist stores are all owned by the same companies and are a front for nefarious businesses.

We recommend shopping for quality, not quantity. Sure, you need to pick up some postcards and whatnot, but focus instead on getting unique gifts that you won't be able to get anywhere else – gifts that will sit on a shelf and be admired or have a good story. That can mean good finds in a market or antique store.

If you really want some tatty souvenirs, then save your souvenir shopping for the airport. There are ample stores there where you can buy all that neat stuff tax-free instead.

OFFICIAL LICENSED PR

LOND

Size **M**

WESTMINSTER
NATIONAL
GALLER ABBEY
THE MALL
LONDON
EYE
BIG BEN
K S
GARDENS
P L S
T A T
CATHE
DRAL
MODERN
R I
D G E
NELSONS
OLUMN

© 2012

BUCKINGHAM PALACE
BRITISH MUSEUM
THE TOWER OF LONDON

LONDON

73. QUICK CLOTHING SIZE CONVERSIONS

Most clothing and shoe sizes will have the equivalent US size on the labels. As a general guide, women's jeans/ denim waist sizing is the same for the US and the UK. Letter sizing (e.g., S, M, L, XL) is also the same for the US and UK. For example, a US size S (small) is the same as a UK size S.

UK and the US men's clothing share the same clothing sizes for both casual and formal wear. This includes neck size, sleeve length, sport coat/jacket sizing (also called chest size), and waist size.

Men's and women's shoe sizes are different in the US and UK. Measure your feet and try different sizes on to ensure a proper fit.

74. TOP 5 SHOPPING

London is one of the top shopping destinations in the world. We have a few favorite places we like to visit while we're in town. We try to avoid places where we can shop back home as they all have the same products these days. We like to hit chains that aren't in the USA and local stores you won't find anywhere else.

Here's a selection of places where you can do some serious shopping.

1. **Oxford Street** - This is tourist alley, but you'll find all the major British brands as well as big department stores. It will also be very busy.
2. **New Bond Street** - Home to a series of pricey boutiques where it's fun to window shop.
3. **Westfield Malls** - London is now home to two mega Westfield Shopping Malls. There are two locations: White City/Shepherds Bush near the former BBC Headquarters and the other is in Stratford City (where the Olympics were held), which is Europe's largest mall.
4. **Camden Lock Market** - This market is for young people and features the latest urban designs and young designers. It's a bustling market that sprawls over several areas that all have their own distinct feel. Also, a great place to eat!
5. **Portobello Road Market** - This market is now pretty much geared toward tourists seeking to relive the film Notting Hill. When it takes place on Saturdays, it will be mobbed with tourists, almost to the point where it's hard to walk down the street. That said, it's a fun experience the first time as you find all kinds of cool stuff you won't find anywhere else. Don't expect to find any deals though – it's tourist priced.

75. FASHION CENTRAL

Because it's in Europe, London gets new fashions first before they catch on in America. Girls, take note of what Londonistas are wearing, as the styles will make it to America in the coming months. Check out the local Topshops, Zaras, and FCUKs for the latest fashions that you can export back home. You'll be on the cutting edge of the latest fashion trends.

76. USED BOOKS ON THE THAMES

There's a great used book market located under Waterloo Bridge on the Southbank of the Thames. It's open daily, and we've always found a good selection of books – some that you won't find in the USA. Many of the books have knockdown prices. There's nothing like browsing amongst old books on the banks of the Thames.

77. BEST BOOKSHOPS IN LONDON

Charing Cross Road is legendary for its array of musty old bookstores. Sadly, many have not survived into the 21st Century. But there are still a lot of great used and niche bookstores clustered in Cecil Court, just off Charing Cross Road near Leicester Square.

Here's a list of 6 bookstores worth visiting in the area as well.

1. **Gosh!** - Comic Books and graphic novel store in Soho
2. **Foyle's Books** - One of the best bookstores in London recently opened a beautiful new megastore on Shaftesbury Avenue.
3. **Forbidden Planet** - Geek haven in Central London on Shaftesbury Avenue.
4. **Hatchard's of Piccadilly** – The oldest bookstore in London. It's stately! The kind of bookstore you imagine London should have.
5. **Stanfords** - While the new location in Covent Garden doesn't have the same Edwardian splendor, this is still the best travel bookstore in the world!

78. HARRODS SHOPPING TIPS

Harrods almost deserves its own dedicated day in any London itinerary. Here are a few tips to make the most of your time in the world's most famous department store.

- Harrods has different hours on Sunday (they used to just be closed): 11:30 am – 6 pm.
- Their regular hours are Mon-Sat 10 am – 9 pm.
- There is a variety of places to eat in Harrods, including sushi, tea, sandwich shops, and more.
- There is a dress code. You must look clean and presentable, or they may not let you in (they didn't let Madonna in once!). No torn jeans, sweatpants, etc. Their website has more details.
- You need to pay before you leave a particular department. It may be one big store, but it's more like a mall with separate shops.
- There's a Harrods shop at the airport that has most of the major souvenirs and expensive designer goods, and it is tax-free there.
- If you spend £100 or more, you can claim back your VAT on the spot (20% of your purchase!). Big savings!
- They will let you pay in US dollars at the till, but we do not recommend doing so as you will not get the best exchange rate. Best to pay in cash or credit card in pounds sterling.

79. VERY OLD STORES

London is one of the oldest cities on the planet, and there are several stores that have been operating for many hundreds of years. Here's a quick list of a few worth visiting.

1. **Twinings Tea Store since 1717** - The original home for Twinings Tea and they do tours and tastings.
2. **Lock & Co Hatters since 1676** - They sell the best English-style hats money can buy (with prices to match!).
3. **James Smith & Sons since 1830** - They make and sell custom umbrellas and it's a fun store to browse.
4. **The Old Curiosity Shop since 1666** - They sell curiosities and are famous for their connection to the Dickens story.
5. **Hamley's Toy Store since 1760** - London's toy mecca. A must-see if you have children.
6. **Hatchards of Piccadilly** - The oldest bookstore in London since 1795.

80. TOP 5 BLOOMSBURY

This genteel and quiet area of London is home to world-class museums and famous for its literary connections.

1. **British Museum** - No trip to London is complete without a visit to the British Museum. Give yourself plenty of time to explore.
2. **Russell Square** - Relax amongst the giant old trees in our favorite quiet London square.
3. **Cartoon Museum** - See the history of the art behind cartooning.
4. **British Library** - Britain's national library. Don't miss the Magna Carta.
5. **Senate House** - Stunning art-deco architecture at the University of London.

81. TOP 5 SOUTHBANK

The South Bank of the River Thames is a vibrant and fun area to spend time in. It's one of our favorite places in London. Here are five things we love to do.

1. **London Eye** - A must for any first-time visitor to London. It will help orient you geographically. You really only need to do it once, though.
2. **Tate Modern** - We're more into the building itself than the art inside, but worth a visit.
3. **Imperial War Museum** - Dedicated to Britain's Empire and the wars it fought. Not to be missed.
4. **National Theatre** - Take in a show at the recently renovated National Theatre.
5. **Globe Theatre** - Take a tour of the reconstructed Globe Theatre, and stay for a play.

82. WATCH OUT FOR PICKPOCKETS!

I know that sounds like travel advice from the 1880s, but believe it or not, they're everywhere in London, and they prey on American tourists (who are easily identified).

Don't carry all your money with you or your passport. Keep ID and money in a buttoned pocket or a pocket with Velcro, so you'll notice if someone tries to pickpocket you.

We've been pickpocketed (thankfully, there was nothing for them to steal!), and it's not a pleasant experience. The thieves are usually gone right after you realize you were just pickpocketed.

Most travelers these days don't carry much cash, but credit cards can still be stolen and used, and they're very hard to replace when you're traveling abroad. Always a good idea to leave a spare credit card with your valuables in your room.

83. ON PUBLIC TOILETS

London is home to a ton of free and paid public toilets. Many businesses don't have toilets accessible to the public (which is considered a right in the USA), so the city makes up for it by providing paid facilities throughout the capital.

They're obviously a useful convenience when you're "caught short" (as the British say). Some are free to use, and others charge a fee. Paying to use a public toilet is rather a strange concept for Americans to get used to, but once you realize it pays for security and cleanliness, it's worth the few pence you have to pay.

Keep in mind, though, that the free public toilets will be magnets for less than savory characters, especially at night in places like Leicester Square. We've been scared to death by drug addicts and crazies on several journeys around London at night. We recommend avoiding public conveniences at night.

The railway stations used to charge for toilet use, but that has been phased out. The major terminus railway stations have large and clean bathrooms. Most Tube stations do not have a public restroom; neither do many small restaurants and cafés. When you have a chronic restroom related condition, this can get quite stressful. So, I like to keep a mental inventory of where I know there are accessible public restrooms.

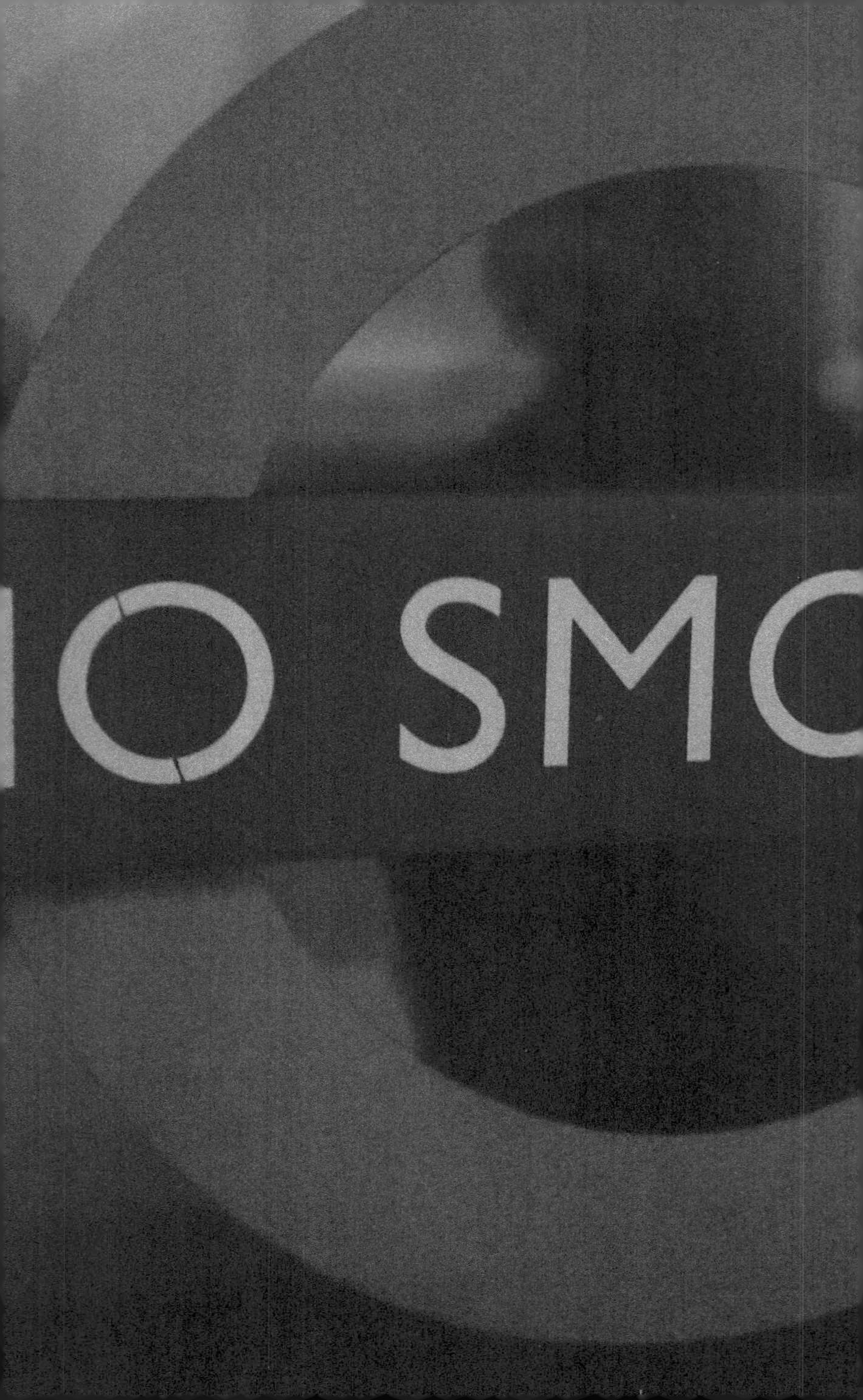
O SM

84. LONDON IS SMOKE-FREE!

There is pretty much no smoking anywhere indoors in London, including pubs. The days of the smoky pub are now extinct.

It's great - you no longer have to sit in the smoking/non-smoking section, and places like Gordon's Wine Bar are no longer so smoky it's uncomfortable.

People still vape, though, which is annoying, and many people will stand uncomfortably close to the entrances of places and smoke - still forcing you to travel through a cloud of smoke.

85. NATIONAL HEALTH SERVICE FOR TOURISTS

Yes, the UK has free healthcare. However, foreigners traveling in the UK don't have unlimited access to it. If you have an emergency, you don't have to worry about paying a bill. If you require longer care, they can and will bill you. It's a good idea to take out travel insurance if you're worried about your health while abroad. Travel Insurance will help ensure you get all the care you would require.

Do not be afraid to go to a British hospital if you have an emergency. You will get treated with the same quality of care you would get back home.

They call their emergency rooms "Accident & Emergency" – often just shortened to A&E (not the TV channel).

If you have a medical emergency, dial **999** – that's the British version of 911. If you have a medical question and it's not an emergency, you can call 111 for the NHS Direct Line for help. If you need a prescription filled, contact a local pharmacy, and they can help you.

CHANGE GIVEN

35

Touch scre

Change Given

Please pay: £5.00

You are being sold
how you to you go balance

£5.20

or notes, or bank card

Back To
Left Screen   Canc

86. GET AN OYSTER CARD

An Oyster Card is an electronic card used across the Tube network, on buses, trams, DLR, London Overground, TfL Rail, River Bus and most National Rail services in London. See the Transport for London website tfl.gov.uk for full details. Note that London buses are all cashless, so you need to use an Oyster card, Travelcard or contactless payment.

You swipe your Oyster card to get through the gates at any Tube station, and tap it when getting on a bus or tram. It's a much quicker way to travel across the network than using tickets, and it's very popular.

It's popular because you always get the lowest fare possible when you use it. If you use the Tube or bus several times during the day, you won't pay more than a certain price for your entire day of journeys. Use of the Oyster card is also heavily discounted – you save over 50% versus paying cash for a ticket.

Before you leave for London, buy a Visitor Oyster card. It's much cheaper than buying a day or week pass. You can purchase them easily from the Visit Britain website, or you can also buy one in London, but it's easier to do so before you get there. They're pretty much good forever, I've had mine for over a decade and just refill it when I'm in London.

London's transport system also supports contactless credit cards (the kind you can hover or tap,) and you can access the network with just one of those, bypassing the need for an Oyster Card. Your usage will still be tracked, and at the end of the day you'll be charged the lowest fare for all your use.

87. LONDON TRANSPORT OPERATING HOURS

This is the biggest change since we published the first edition of this guidebook. There is now a Night Tube 24 hour service on some Tube lines. The rest of the Tube closes after midnight and opens around 5 am depending on the line. If you plan to be out late, and you don't have a Night Tube line, you'll need to rely on London Black Taxis or the bus to get back to your hotel.

The bus system runs 24 hours, so you can always rely on that to get where you need to go. Buses are also cheaper than the Tube, and you'll get more local color this way.

You can expect London Black Taxis to operate through the night, but they will become harder to find them the later (and earlier) it gets. Avoid minicabs at all costs as they are unlicensed and don't require the training that Black Cab drivers have. We've also had strange experiences when looking for a cab where random people will offer us a ride. Don't ever do this.

Uber and other ride-sharing apps have completely changed this; you can now hire a cab from your phone pretty much anywhere safely.

88. AVOID COVENT GARDEN TUBE

Leicester Square Tube Station and Covent Garden Tube Station are literally several hundred feet from each other, but Leicester Square can handle the crowds better.

If you want to go to Covent Garden, get off at Leicester Square, and walk up Longacre to Covent Garden. There are signs to direct you.

Covent Garden Tube has very slow elevators, and the crowds build up very quickly in this popular tourist area. There are also too many stairs to climb (the signs tell you this).

89. GETTING FROM THE AIRPORTS

The Heathrow Express to London Paddington Station is the quickest and easiest way to get into central London from the airport. It's rather expensive, but it's quiet and a nice ride after a long flight. It drops you right in the middle of everything, and it's easy to get transport to your hotel from Paddington.

The Gatwick Express operates similarly to the Heathrow Express, but it takes a little longer as Gatwick is further away from London.

The Tube is the cheapest way to get to London from Heathrow but takes three times as long as it has to make all the stops.

There are regular buses from the airport to Central London, but these will be much slower than the Tube. So, take the Tube!

We would avoid taking a cab from the airport, as you'll spend about $100 on cab fare – money much better spent on your entertainment in London itself rather than getting there.

90. GETTING TO PARIS

High-Speed trains to Paris depart from St. Pancras station, and it takes just 2 hours 15 minutes to get there. If you're this close, why not go for the day? It will be worth it.

A day trip to Paris is a great way to experience the city but not have to stay there. You can see most of the major sites, have dinner at a café, and be back in London in time for bed.

A Eurostar ticket will cost you about $100 and is well worth the money. Don't even think about flying from London to Paris. It's just not that far, and you'll spend a fortune getting from the airport to central Paris. The Eurostar drops you right in the middle of Paris. The Eurostar also now goes direct to Brussels and Amsterdam.

98. LOST? NEED GUIDANCE?

Pop into one of the London Visitor's Information Centres located around central London. They offer free help and guidance for all your London questions. They'll help you book hotels, theatre tickets, train tickets, etc. They have ample free maps and brochures for the taking. It's an invaluable London resource. See a current list on the Visit London website: https://visitlondon.com/tag/tourist-information-centre

Also download their free app!

99. LONDON SLANG WORDS

One thing you'll notice when you travel to London is all the strange words they use to describe things. Sometimes they make sense, sometimes they don't. To help the wayward tourist, here's a list of words you'll find when you travel to London.

- Tube = London Underground Network
- The Knowledge = Geographical information London's black cab drivers have to learn to be licensed. They have to learn every street in London.
- Boris Bus = When Mayor of London, Boris Johnson's key platform promise was replacing the old London Routemaster bus with a 'new bus for London.'
- The Standard = What some call the Evening Standard – the evening paper dedicated to London.
- The City = The City of London – the square mile bit of central London that goes back two thousand years.
- The Beehive = Nickname for London's City Hall and Assembly building.
- Square Mile = Also the City of London.
- Congestion Charge = Tax on all cars entering the central London congestion charge zone.
- Silicon Roundabout = Area around Old Street that's a

hub for new media and tech companies.
- Council Estate = Public housing
- The Blitz = Period in 1940 when London was bombed by the Nazis.
- M25 = The Orbital Highway that encircles London, considered the 'border' of London (despite the fact it goes beyond it in places).
- Westway = Elevated Highway in West London.
- Mind the Gap = Watch your step when stepping from a train to a platform.
- Buck House = Buckingham Palace
- The Tower = Tower of London
- A-Z = A popular London map guide that's indispensable to locals and long-term visitors (Extra note – Londoners will say "A to Zed").
- GMT = Greenwich Mean Time.
- Cockney = Someone born within earshot of the bells of St Mary-le-Bow.
- Offy, short for Off License = a convenience store which sells alcohol.
- Take Away = Cheap to-go food.
- Crossrail = New cross-London underground railway line currently under construction. As of publication, it's still under construction but will open in the early 2020s.
- Bobby = London policeman.
- Zebra Crossing = Pedestrian crossing.
- Home Counties = Generic name for the counties around London: Bedfordshire, Berkshire, Buckinghamshire, Cambridgeshire, Dorset, Essex, Hampshire, Hertfordshire, Kent, Middlesex, Oxfordshire, Surrey, and Sussex.
- Pissed = Drunk.
- Pants = Underwear or something that sucks.
- Trousers = Pants.
- Quid = Pound.
- Knackered = Tired.
- Loo = Toilet.
- Kip = Sleep/Nap.

- Tenner = £10.
- Nappy Valley = Areas of London with high birthrates like Battersea.
- Chelsea tractor = Slang for Land Rover, an expensive car driven by the rich in London.

100. PLAN THE NEXT DAY THE NIGHT BEFORE

While we do like to leave some things to spontaneity, we do like to the make the most of every minute we're in London. While we generally arrive with a list of things we'd like to do before the trip, we find it's fun to switch things around based on what we're feeling and the weather forecast.

A good tip is to plan your next day the night before. That gives you plenty of time in front of the telly to figure out how to get to all the places you want to go, when they open, and how much they cost. And also plan meal breaks (and maybe even the toilet). This is especially helpful if you plan on travelling anywhere outside central London or need to book tickets for a show.

Get the map out, plot where the places you want to go are and figure out the best way to see it all.

101. THINK OF YOUR LONDON FUTURE!

You will not have enough time to do everything you want to do in London in one trip. Don't even try. We've been to London 20 times now, and we still haven't seen everything we want to see.

There's nothing worse than spending your vacation completely exhausted because you're trying to do it all.

Don't stress, manage your time well, understand that it's a foreign place, and you'll have a fantastic time, and want to return time and time again. Many people think that they only have one chance to go to London. If you've been once, you can most certainly go again.

Happy London Travels!

BONUS APPENDIX

101 FREE THINGS TO DO IN LONDON

Here is a huge list of things that you can do in London for free. We've put a lot of work into this list, and we hope that you can create some lovely London memories by doing some of the things listed. This is a springboard for doing your own research on how to get to each of these places and when they're open.

1. British Museum – The best Museum in London. Plan a whole day here.
2. National Gallery – Some of history's best art for free.
3. Trafalgar Square – Go see Nelson and people-watch as London goes by.
4. Walk through Hyde Park – No trip to London is complete without a walk through Hyde Park.
5. Covent Garden – Explore the old market, watch street performers, hear musicians. Plenty of free fun to be had in Covent Garden!
6. Walk along the Thames – Smell the fresh river air and listen to the Thames lap along the shore.
7. Tate Modern – Some of the art is questionable, but the building is amazing in itself and worth a visit alone.
8. Evensong Church Service – You have to pay admission to get into most of London's cathedrals, but if you go to evensong service, you can get in for free.
9. Cross Tower Bridge – It's a free thrill for all tourists to cross the bridge! Wait around, and you might even see it open and close.

10. National Maritime Museum – Explore the history of Britain's Royal Navy.
11. Walk through the Woolwich Foot Tunnel – Cross one of the oldest tunnels under the Thames – get off the DLR stop King George V and walk to the entrance.
12. Pollocks Toy Museum – Toys from around the world – a great place for the kids!
13. Imperial War Museum – See Britain's military history in all its glory.
14. Borough Market – Explore one of London's coolest markets!
15. British Film Institute's Mediatheque – Explore Britain's film heritage.
16. Houses of Parliament – It costs money to go inside, but that doesn't have to stop you from checking out the building from the outside.
17. Museum of London – Fun look at the history of London.
18. National Portrait Gallery – While many of its pictures are of the aristocracy through the ages, there are also lots of paintings and photographs of celebrities.
19. Natural History Museum – One of the world's finest natural history museums. Check out the Darwin Centre!
20. Victoria and Albert Museum – A strange hodge-podge museum that provides an interesting insight into Britain's cultural heritage.
21. Science Museum – Who doesn't like science? Kids will love it!
22. Serpentine Gallery – Art Gallery located in Hyde Park that rotates various exhibitions throughout the year.
23. Tate Britain – Like the National Gallery, it's home to some beautiful art.
24. Guildhall Art Gallery – Collection of art collected by the Corporation of London.
25. Wallace Collection – Collection of European art and artifacts.
26. Whitechapel Gallery – Modern art gallery in East London.

27. Bank of England Museum – Take a look at the monetary history of the world.
28. Changing of the Guard – It's a tourist trap, but always fun to watch on a sunny day. Every day in the summer at 11:30. Arrive early.
29. The Ceremony of the Keys – Watch the nightly lock-up of the Tower of London. You have to request permission to witness this, but it's pretty cool.
30. Sir John Soane's Museum – The eclectic collection of a famous London architect exactly as he left it.
31. Kenwood House – Lovely stately home located in Hampstead Heath.
32. Geffrye Museum – Period rooms from 1600 to today.
33. Royal Air Force Museum – See the history of Britain's flying aces.
34. Horniman Museum – An eclectic family museum with many different displays.
35. Queen Mary's Rose Garden – London's largest and best rose garden.
36. St James's Park – One of London's fine Royal Parks.
37. The Globe Theatre – See the replica of the theatre that was home to Shakespeare's plays! It costs to get in for a tour, but not to have a look outside.
38. Princess Diana Memorial – Located in Hyde Park, you can pay your respects to Princess Di.
39. Speakers' Corner – Arrive on a Sunday morning, and watch the colorful characters gathered to speak about anything.
40. Leicester Square – Relax in the park in the middle or admire the glitzy lights of this tourist haven.
41. Tower Bridge Lifts – Watch Tower Bridge open and close.
42. Museum of London's Docklands – A lesser-known London, but cool none the less. You explore London's maritime shipping history.
43. Lunch Concerts at St. Martin in the Fields – Enjoy lunch in the Crypt, and also enjoy free concerts every day.
44. Free Concerts at the National Theatre – Check with

them for regular free concerts open to the public.

45. Watch a TV Show Recorded at the BBC – It's free to be in the studio audience of a show as it's being recorded.
46. View London from Primrose Hill – Admire the view from London's Primrose Hill.
47. London Silver Vaults – Check out the world's largest retail collection of fine antique silver.
48. Hunterian Museum – See a unique collection of animal specimens kept in jars.
49. Watch a Trial at Central Criminal Court – It's free to watch a trial take place from the public galleries.
50. Walk through the City on a Saturday – The Square Mile or City of London is practically abandoned on the weekends. Check out the cool architecture and enjoy the quiet streets.
51. Street Performers in Covent Garden or the South Bank – Seek out buskers throughout London for free and fun entertainment.
52. Catch a Film Premiere in Leicester Square – The Odeon Theatre regularly holds film premieres where you can catch a glimpse of stars.
53. Coram's Fields – Unique seven-acre playground and park for children living in or visiting London.
54. Foundling Museum – Britain's original home for abandoned children and London's first-ever public art gallery.
55. The Photographers' Gallery – Largest public display gallery dedicated to photography.
56. Peter Pan Statue – Check out the statue of the literary classic located in Kensington Gardens.
57. Museum of Childhood – Dedicated to the history of childhood.
58. See the London Stone – Check out the Roman Stone from where all distance from London is measured located at 111 Cannon Street.
59. Touch the Roman Wall – Throughout the city of London, you'll see traces of the original Roman Wall fortification. There are large pieces around the Museum of London.
60. Check out Piccadilly Circus – See the iconic bright lights

and the famous statue of Eros.

61. Musicians in Covent Garden Apple Market – On the lower levels of the Market, there are usually musicians busking while people eat.

62. Explore Leadenhall Market – Gorgeous market located in the City of London worth exploring for the architecture alone.

63. Walk Across Hampstead Heath – Beautiful park in London that provides lovely views of metropolitan London.

64. Visit Regent's Park – Another great Royal Park, and there's a zoo!

65. Wellington Arch – One of two triumphal arches in London.

66. Marble Arch – The second triumphal arch in London.

67. Visit Platform 9 3/4 – Doesn't really exist, of course, but station authorities have set up a fake entrance for Harry Potter fans at King's Cross Station.

68. Visit St Pancras International – Admire this beautiful station, watch Eurostar trains arrive and depart, and visit the statue of the couple kissing.

69. Free Music at the Notting Hill Arts Club – Regular free music in Notting Hill.

70. Harrod's Food Hall – Browse quail eggs, cava, and custom-made cakes in the sumptuous food halls in Harrods.

71. Walk along the South Bank – Walk from Waterloo Bridge to the Tate Modern, and see a huge part of London.

72. Walk through Richmond Park – Another lovely park.

73. Changing of the Guard in Windsor – If you happen to be in Windsor, there's a changing of the guard there as well as at Buckingham Palace.

74. Visit Bushy Park – Yet another lovely park.

75. 5th View Bar – Check out the priceless views.

76. Canals of Maida Vale/Little Venice – See London's waterways and cute boats where people actually live!

77. Abbey Road Crosswalk – Become a traffic hazard, and have your own Beatles pictures taken.

78. Admire the Barbican – Built after World War II, it's a

triumph of modernism.

79. Postman's Park – The square from the movie "Closer" where memorials are dedicated to people who died saving Londoners.

80. Take a free London guided walk – Pick up a guidebook or download a free audio tour, and do your own London walk.

81. Notting Hill Bookshop – Visit the bookstore that the shop in the film Notting Hill was based on, which used to be called The Travel Bookshop.

82. Portobello Road Market – Be prepared for huge crowds, but no visit to London is complete without experiencing the bustling market.

83. Explore Blue Plaques – Look closely at old buildings, and you'll see lots of blue plaques, which offer some history about famous people who lived there.

84. Listen to Big Ben chime – Stand in Parliament Square at noon and wait for Big Ben to make its music.

85. Visit the New U.S. Embassy – You can't go inside unless you have business, but you can admire the new building and the beautiful gardens that surround it.

86. Visit the Cenotaph – Pay respects at Britain's memorial to the two World Wars.

87. Explore Camden Town and Camden Lock Market – Much bigger than Portobello Road and much more to see.

88. Check out City Hall and the Scoop – Admire London's bee-hive-shaped City Hall and watch out for free performances in the Scoop outside.

89. Visit 10 Downing Street – Get a glimpse of the residence of the Prime Minister. Wait long enough, and you might see him come and go.

90. Picnic in Battersea Park – Lovely riverside park with views of the Thames.

91. Cross the Jubilee Bridge – Cross the Thames at Embankment on this beautiful bridge.

92. Cross the Millennium Bridge – Best way to cross from the Tate Modern to St Paul's or vice versa.

93. See the Roosevelt & Churchill Statue – Located in Bond Street, see the two great world leaders as friends.
94. See the Churchill Statue – Located in Parliament Square.
95. See the Lincoln Statue – Statue of the American president located in Parliament Square. The only one to have such an honor.
96. Free WiFi in the Apple Stores – Need WiFi or access to the web? Then stop in the Apple Stores in Covent Garden or Regent Street and recharge your Internet batteries.
97. Get photographed in a red phone box – Nothing more touristy or more awesome than a picture in a red phone box.
98. Visit the National Army Museum – Discover the history of Britain's armed forces.
99. Visit Russell Square – Quiet little green park in the middle of bustling London right around the corner from the British Museum.
100. Visit the 7-7 Memorial – Located in Hyde Park on the east side; you can pay your respects to those who lost their lives in the terror attacks on 7-7-05.
101. Feed the Ducks in St James Park – They'll appreciate it!

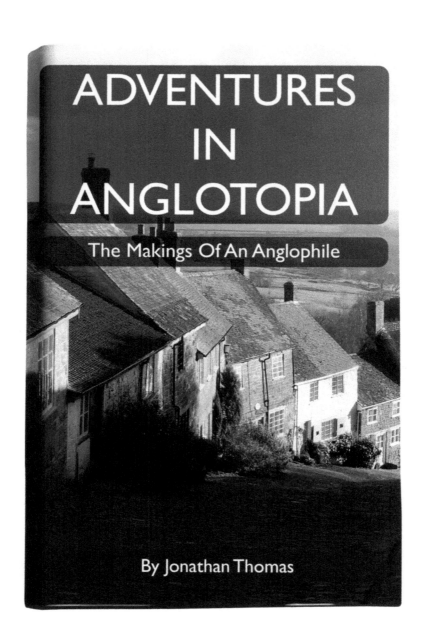

ADVENTURES IN ANGLOTOPIA

The Makings Of An Anglophile

By Jonathan Thomas

Now Available from Booksellers Everywhere

Adventures in Anglotopia
The Makings Of An Anglophile

By Jonathan Thomas

What makes an Anglophile? What makes someone love a country not their own? Adventures in Anglotopia is a journey to answer this question, framed through a childhood exposed to British culture and then nearly twenty years of travel in Britain. It's an exploration of why one American man loves Britain so much but also why Britain is such a wonderful place, worthy of loving unconditionally.

The narrative arc of the book answers this question by covering interesting topics related to Britain such as visiting for the first time, culture, stately home, tea, history, British TV, literature, specific places, and much more. Each chapter focuses on a specific topic, all building to the end where Jonathan reveals his 'Great British Dream.'

Come on a journey that will take you the length and breadth of Britain and its rich history.

ISBN: 978-0985477080

Available from all bookstores and direct from Anglotopia at
http://adventuresinanglotopia.com

About Anglotopia.net

Anglotopia.net is the world's largest website for people who love Britain. Founded in 2007, it has grown to be the biggest community of passionate Anglophiles anywhere. With daily updates covering British Culture, History, and Travel - Anglotopia is the place to get your British Fix!

https://anglotopia.net
https://londontopia.net